EUCHA
DEVOTION

New Meanings
for a Timeless Tradition

EUCHARISTIC DEVOTION

New Meanings for a Timeless Tradition

Bernard Häring, C.SS.R.

LIGUORI
PUBLICATIONS

One Liguori Drive
Liguori, Missouri 63057
(314) 464-2500

Imprimi Potest:
James F. Dowd, C.SS.R.
Provincial, St. Louis Province
The Redemptorists

Imprimatur:
+ Edward J. O'Donnell
Vicar General, Archdiocese of St. Louis

ISBN 0-89243-261-6
Library of Congress Catalog Card Number: 86-83009

Table of Contents

- "This is the cup of my blood, the blood of the new and everlasting covenant"
- "So that sins may be forgiven"
- "Mystery of Faith"
- "Every time you eat this bread and drink this cup, you proclaim the death of the Lord, until he comes"
- "Adorers in spirit and in truth"

Introduction

The suggestion to write this booklet came to me from the Redemptorists at Liguori Publications, who know that I share their concern for an authentic revival of those traditional Eucharistic devotions which emphasize our Lord's presence flowing from the celebration of the Mass to every dimension of our Christian life.

Most people wholeheartedly agree with the Second Vatican Council's liturgical changes in the celebration of Mass, and they appreciate the postconciliar efforts that encourage active participation by all the faithful. But they are confused when they experience in their parishes or religious communities an almost total abandonment of various forms of Eucharistic veneration which meant so much to their spiritual growth. For example, they miss the Forty Hours Devotion which, through the years, had become the highlight of enthusiastic participation in their parishes and sometimes unforgettable turning points in their lives of faith. And their concern is based not on mere sentimentalism; it is a result of their sorrow in the face of a very real loss.

Five years after the end of the Council, I closed a retreat for a good number of nuns from various congregations with solemn exposition of the Blessed Sacrament and solemn

7

blessing. To my surprise, several nuns came to tell me how much they had missed this devotion since the Council.

It does not disturb me to see that, in many churches, the tabernacle has been removed from the main altar to a side altar or to a special side chapel. But what really worries me is that even priests and religious in some parts of the Catholic world have almost completely abandoned their visits to the Blessed Sacrament, and seem not to feel the need or miss the joy of responding to the Lord's gracious permanent presence in the tabernacle.

People become even more confused when they adopt the wrong impression that the Holy See and the Council actually intended these changes. One of the purposes of this booklet is to show that Vatican II intended no such thing.

In 1965, in full agreement with the Second Vatican Council, Pope Paul VI emphasized in his encyclical, *Mystery of Faith,* the real and permanent presence of the Lord in the Eucharist and pointed out the importance of devotions which surround the reservation of the Eucharist. In May, 1967, the Holy See issued a document entitled *Instruction on Eucharistic Worship,* which helped Catholics to better understand the history of the Eucharist and the deeper meanings of its devotional forms. And with the same purpose in mind — to promote a sound revival of Eucharistic veneration — Pope John Paul II published, in 1980, his letter to all bishops, *On the Mystery and Worship of the Eucharist.*

Based on these documents and on notable studies of the history, theology, and spirituality of Eucharistic worship, these pages are written to encourage those who — despite opposition — have persevered in practicing their beloved Eucharistic devotions with enthusiasm. It is also hoped that those who are confused in this matter will learn from this booklet a better understanding of the history and the profound meaning of the various forms of Eucharistic devotions.

May I share with my readers two special reasons for my personal interest in this topic? During World War II, I served as a medic for the German soldiers at the Russian front. Although I was a priest, I was not a military chaplain. Since I had to care for many wounded and dying people — military and civilian — I always carried with me the Eucharistic species; and many, many times I saw the immense consolation I was able to give these people when I would tell them, ''I am a priest,'' and could give them Holy Communion at the hour of their death. Those difficult years provided me with countless opportunities to become more deeply acquainted with Jesus, our Way, our Life, the Consoler of the sick and dying.

A second reason is my Redemptorist vocation, which makes me a son of Saint Alphonsus, one of the great venerators of the Blessed Sacrament. Further, the writings of Sister Celeste Crostarosa, the foundress of the Order of Redemptoristines, had a great impact on my own vision of Christian life as living the history of salvation with a ''Eucharistic memory.''

We can never praise the Lord enough for his great testament, the Eucharist, and his abiding presence among us. We join the angels and saints in their unending praise. And we hope that this booklet will inspire each reader to make his or her life an expression of Eucharistic praise.

I

History
of Eucharistic
Devotion

Holy Scripture provides us with ample evidence of the Eucharist as the Lord's testament, as memorial, as sign of abiding presence, source of life eternal, sign of unity, and proclamation of Christ's death and Resurrection until he comes in glory. As for devotions founded on Christ's Eucharistic presence, the history of the Church gives us pertinent information, and the teaching authority of the Church provides guidance for present practice in this area. Here we will consider the history of the Eucharistic celebration and especially the devotions which developed as a result of our Lord's presence on the altar.

The Mass: Center and Summit of Christian Community

The teaching of the Church provides abundant evidence that the celebration of the Eucharistic memorial — as sacrifice and meal — is absolutely vital for the life of the Church and particularly for all the other forms of Eucharistic devotion.

The *Constitution on the Sacred Liturgy* and the postconciliar liturgical renewal have brought this home to all the faithful. This renewal has also furthered the ecumenical movement, since the Eastern Orthodox churches and the ecclesiastical communities born of the sixteenth-century Reformation were extremely critical about certain forms of the Eucharistic cult. Both the Eastern Orthodox and Protestant Churches felt that Catholic liturgical practice had become unfaithful to the biblical doctrine on the Eucharist, particularly overemphasizing Eucharistic devotions to the detriment of the Eucharistic celebration of the Lord's Supper.

Most expressions of Eucharistic worship, as we knew it

before the Second Vatican Council, were unknown during the first thousand years of the Church. And, when new forms developed in and after the eleventh century, the Church authorities consistently rejected any practice that might overshadow the centrality of the Eucharistic celebration as such. From the eleventh to the thirteenth centuries, the practice of distributing Communion outside the Eucharistic celebration was introduced in many parts of the Western Church. This new practice was often censured but later tolerated only as an exception. Good theology explained Communion outside Mass to be in conformity with the ancient Christian practice.

From the earliest times, there were many cases of reception of Communion outside the direct celebration of the Mass. During the first centuries, the faithful could bring Holy Communion to the sick, especially to the dying, but also to others who were unable to participate in the celebration of Mass. It was clearly understood, however, that this practice was meant to bring them a share of the Eucharistic memorial, the great sign of unity. Thus, those who received the Eucharistic species at home felt included in the Eucharistic sacrifice. We shall see later that, already during the first centuries, there were exceptions. Especially in times of persecution, the faithful could keep the reserved species in their homes for several days.

The history of the Eucharist records many innovations which, however, did not survive. One of the best documented practices of this kind was an effort to emphasize the unity of all parishes with the bishop or the unity of bishops with the successor of Peter. Innocent I, in 416, writes in a letter to Bishop Decentius of Gubbio about the practice of "fermentum": immediately after the Mass celebrated by the bishop of Rome, acolytes are to bring consecrated species to the churches in the neighborhood, not for reservation but for use at the moment when, during the Mass, the consecrated bread is mixed with the consecrated wine. The "fermentum" was distributed only five times a year: on Thursday and Saturday of Holy Week, and on Easter, Pentecost, and Christmas.

During the eighth century, the pope gave to each newly consecrated bishop the Eucharistic bread from which he could receive Communion during the following forty days. Bishops in France did the same for the newly ordained priests. These priests celebrated their own Mass but used the "fermentum" for the mixture of the consecrated species, as a sign of unity with the bishop. However, these practices never became universal and they eventually died out. Although they in no way opposed the centrality of the Eucharistic celebration as such — since they were meant only to emphasize unity in the celebration — they were, in the eyes of many, inappropriate expressions.

Reservation of the Eucharist: Viaticum and Communion for the Sick

The most ancient, best documented, and most relevant forms of reservation of the Eucharistic species were the Viaticum and Communion for the sick. Here we have the most evident testimony of faith in the permanent presence of the Lord in the consecrated Host and the most convincing argument for preserving the consecrated species.

The oldest form of Viaticum is the "home Communion," where there was either a Mass in the sick person's house or — more commonly — a member of the family or another lay person brought the consecrated Host directly from the Eucharistic celebration to the sufferer. During a long period of history the consecrated species could be preserved in the home of a gravely sick person so that he or she could receive Communion, especially on the last day or hour of life. From the fourth century on, however, the more common form was to bring or send the Viaticum directly from the Eucharistic celebration or to distribute it within a home Mass. Later, in many places, a few Eucharistic species were preserved in the sanctuary, in the sacristy, or in the priest's house — to be used for emergency sick calls.

From the eleventh century onward, the solemn rite of Viaticum developed more and more. The one who carried the Viaticum was often joined by a pious procession of many people. We shall return later to the many ways in which the Church, throughout the ages, strove to make sure that Viaticum was available for all the faithful. Here we witness a most moving dimension of Eucharistic devotion: welcoming, revering, loving the divine Visitor coming to the sick and dying.

The Eucharist: Companion on Journeys and in Times of Distress

Jesus assures us that he is the Way and that if we trust in him he will accompany us on our way in this valley of tears. From this, many Christians drew the conclusion that they acted in accord with Jesus' intentions when they kept with them the Eucharistic species on long and dangerous journeys. The consecrated bread, which they hung around their necks, served as a safeguard for the journey and provided assurance of receiving the Viaticum in danger of death. There are only a few documents from the fourth to the eighth centuries about this custom, but such a practice at that time was not astonishing since preservation of the Eucharist by the laity was not yet universally forbidden. In the Eastern Churches, hermits and stylites were allowed to have the

Eucharist with them as their permanent "companion" and thus have it available as their Viaticum in their final hour.

Throughout the Middle Ages it was not unusual, during crusades and on the battlefield, for a priest — even at the front — to carry the Body of Christ. But there was never a universal law allowing or encouraging the practice.

From the fourteenth to the eighteenth centuries, several popes, when journeying, took the Eucharist with them in solemn procession. The pope, riding in his carriage, was preceded by a white horse carrying on his back a tabernacle which held the consecrated wafer. In this case the motivation was quite different. The custom was influenced by the Corpus Christi procession, with the pope coming "in the name of the Lord." Benedict XIII seems to be the last pope who conducted his journeys in this way.

There is also an old tradition which, indeed, has never died out. During times of persecution the Eucharist was sent to those in prison. Those in danger of death (martyrs-to-be) also were allowed to have the consecrated Host with them. And there are moving accounts of people taking extreme risks to bring the Eucharistic Host to those imprisoned in concentration camps during our own century.

Further Development of Eucharistic Devotion

No learned Protestant theologian would maintain what sixteenth-century Protestant reformers asserted: They condemned any form of Eucharistic devotion — other than the Lord's Supper itself — as idolatry. It is true that the first eleven or twelve centuries of Church history reveal only traces of these devotions. But there was a gradual development of Eucharistic devotion at this time. Numerous documents from the first centuries indicate a great reverence for our Lord's presence in the Eucharist, even though it was not reserved in a tabernacle for adoration.

During those first centuries when the laity were allowed to bring the Eucharistic Host to their homes and to reserve it there for the sick or for daily Communion, there was always a great emphasis on reverence, on adoration of the Lord before receiving him in Communion, and on great care for the safety of the consecrated species.

Throughout the ages, however, tension did develop in different areas over proper care for the safety of the Host, and for responsible manifestation of reverence. Furthermore, there was not always and everywhere unanimous agreement on what reverence required or allowed. For instance, in some parts of the East the conviction prevailed that reverence for the Lord's sacramental presence required that if some consecrated Hosts remained after being brought from Mass as Viaticum, they should be burned or buried in the earth. However, other voices in the Church maintained that this procedure manifested irreverence. The latter opinion finally prevailed everywhere.

Until the ninth century, during times of persecution and even during peaceful times, in some sectors of the Church the Eucharistic Host was entrusted to the laity and reserved in private homes. Later, only clergy — normally priests — were responsible for this custody, and only very few consecrated species were allowed to be reserved for Viaticum. It was not until centuries later that the Sacrament was reserved for distribution outside the Mass and explicitly for the greater devotion of the worshipers.

For a long time the Eucharist was reserved either in the priest's house or the sacristy or some other place where it could be protected. Here the emphasis was evidently on safety — to prevent attempts at sacrilegious abuse. The tension between concern for the safety of the reserved Eucharist and easy access to Jesus' sacramental presence for the people has continued down through the ages. Like many other Catholics, I am always disappointed when a parish church is locked almost all day. However, while knowledge of the history does not remove a feeling of disappointment, it does make for a greater tolerance and mutual understanding.

During the tenth century, the Eucharist was usually reserved in the sacristy. However, when public veneration of the Blessed Sacrament increased in many parts of the Church in the eleventh century, the privileged place of reservation gradually came to be an ornamental cubicle in the main church. Later on, this tabernacle received ever more artistic attention, although in Italy, for a long time, the sacristy remained the preferred place of reservation; in Milan, because of the influence of Saint Charles Borromeo, this was so until the latter part of the fifteenth century.

Many churches had beautiful sacrament-chapels with ornate tabernacles. The altar-tabernacle, at least in the sense of the tabernacle placed on the main altar, was an exception until much later. And in many cases, Church legislation discouraged reservation of the Hosts on the main altar, where the Eucharistic sacrifice was usually celebrated. This was done, however, not to oppose Eucharistic devotion or to discourage adoration of the Blessed Sacrament in silent prayer. The reasons centered neither on safety nor Eucharistic devotion, but rather on the fact that the altar is the place of Eucharistic sacrifice. In Rome, this tradition was very strong. There was never a tabernacle on the main altar, especially in the great papal basilicas. There were, and still are, beautiful sacrament-chapels within the basilicas, however.

Many of us still remember the former rules of fast before Holy Communion, which dated back to the third century and were probably introduced even earlier. The legal prescriptions underwent many changes and sometimes caused undue scrupulosity. As a young priest, I frequently had to observe complete fasting until afternoon, after I heard confessions, celebrated Mass, and taught catechism in various places. I did not mind this as long as it did not hamper my ministry. It was, among other things, a reminder to look forward to the great moment of Holy Communion. But the change in regulation was timely. Missionary and native-born priests in Africa told me that under the rigid legislation they could celebrate Mass only in the early morning because their health would have suffered terribly if, in the hot climate, they could not have taken water during the day. Unfortunately, the moralists had not taught them the traditional doctrine on *epikeia* (presumption that a law does not apply in case of hardship) or had denied, without good reason, its application to the Eucharistic fast.

Full Development of Eucharistic Devotion Dating from the Eleventh Century

It is a puzzling fact that, in spite of the firm faith in the permanent presence of the Lord in the consecrated species, and in spite of the great reverence evoked by it in the first ten centuries, there was no noticeable development of a public Eucharistic rite outside the celebration of the Eucharistic memorial. Beginning in the eleventh century, certain forms of Eucharistic piety and cult began to develop, but for several centuries the main reason given for reservation of the Blessed Sacrament was only the Viaticum. For example, as late as 1346, a synod in Florence speaks only of the Viaticum as reason for reserving the sacrament. And the statutes of Bishop Wenceslaus in Breslau, 1410, forbade, except on the feast of Corpus Christi, the reservation of the Blessed Sacrament for any reason other than Communion of the sick.

Instructions from the Holy See in 1949 and in 1967 follow the ancient tradition, indicating that the main reason for the reservation of the Blessed Sacrament was its use as Viaticum. But this was and is no reason to belittle other reasons, such as people's fervent prayer and adoration before the tabernacle.

The introduction in the thirteenth century of the elevation of the Host at Mass after the consecration and before the Our Father brought on further development of Eucharistic worship. The faithful took to heart the words of the psalmist, "my eyes are turning toward the Lord," and were thus led to a deep and fervent cult of adoration. Many people began to experience great consolation during the exposition of the Blessed Sacrament.

Great saints, such as Bernard of Clairvaux and Francis of Assisi, were tireless promoters of Eucharistic devotion in its various forms. In 1209, Juliana, a pious nun of Liège began to promote the liturgical celebration of the feast of Corpus Christi. It was officially celebrated for the first time at Liège in 1247, and in 1264 it was given formal approval by Pope Urban IV.

II

Main Dimensions of the Eucharistic Memorial

In our study of the history of the Eucharist and Eucharistic devotion, from its early beginnings until the Second Vatican Council, one of the most evident facts is the centrality and normative value of the Eucharistic memorial, the Mass. Therefore, before reflecting on the various forms of Eucharistic devotion, we must look first to the main dimensions of the Eucharist itself.

First of all, it is the memorial which Christ gave us on the eve of his death, when he said, "Do this in memory of me." It is the solemn assurance of his abiding, life-giving presence — "I shall be with you" — bringing us into intimate contact with his saving sacrifice: "This is my body given for you, my blood shed for you." It provides a redeeming entrance into the company of the "Lamb of God" who destroys the vicious circle of violence, enmity, and treachery. It is a covenantal sharing: "This is the cup of my blood, the blood of the new and everlasting covenant." It emphasizes the importance of conversion: "So that sins may be forgiven." It is the "mystery of faith" which enkindles in us a joyful, grateful faith, and builds up the faith-community: "Every time you eat this bread and drink this cup you proclaim the death of the Lord until he comes." And finally, the Eucharist has the power to make us, in Christ, "adorers in spirit and in truth."

"Do this in memory of me"

The Eucharist is a most distinctive memorial. Recalling the greatest event of God's self-revealing and self-giving love, we praise the Lord, who most graciously remembers us. He calls for our grateful memory of him.

By the Eucharistic testament given to his disciples, Jesus assures us that he will always remember us and wants to be with us whenever, as a community of disciples, we gather to remember his death and Resurrection. By this inimitable memorial he teaches us the relevance of memory, brings our faulty memory up to the level of a Eucharistic one, filled with grateful recollection of all of God's saving works, all his gifts, and all his promises.

The Eucharistic memorial is not just a one-time memento, not just a human effort to recall an event. It is the Lord himself who, by his powerful presence, reminds us that the love with which he gave himself up on the cross is solemnly guaranteed by his Eucharistic testament. All this calls for a most generous response on our part.

While God assures us that he will always be gracious and keep his promise of mercy, he sends us his Spirit to ensure that each member of the community remembers in the proper spirit. The memorial is rightly celebrated when we learn to remember and to celebrate the entire history of salvation, all the works of God, in the focal light of the death and Resurrection of Christ who, by this very memorial, makes us sharers in the event and in the fruits of his Paschal Mystery.

This brings us to a new vision, a new understanding and appreciation of the Incarnation of the Word of God, of Jesus' life and all that happened to his flock since his death, Resurrection, and Ascension into heaven. The lives of Christians who, day by day, relive gratefully the history of salvation — through a Eucharistic memory — give clear evidence of this. It gives cohesion and coherence to their way of life.

Through the Eucharistic memorial, Jesus reminds us that, in the name of all the redeemed, he is present forever to the Father as total gift of himself, pleading for us; and at the same time he is present to us, always ready to give the wonderful gift of himself. Our capacity to receive Christ as total gift depends mainly on the quality of our memory. Is it a healthy, grateful memory or an impoverished one? The Divine Healer makes himself present in the memorial also to heal what we remember. We cannot make a generous and loving response unless we develop a thankful and forgiving memory. Further, we cannot tune in on the wavelength of this wonderful memorial unless we long to respond to the self-giving love of Jesus by a grateful response, entrusting ourselves entirely to him.

The Eucharistic memorial leads to all-encompassing thanksgiving. Rendering thanks, Jesus takes the bread, saying, "Take this, all of you, and eat it: this is my body. . . . " And again he says of the wine: "This is the cup of my blood. . . . " The changing of bread and wine into his body and blood recalls the fact that Jesus was truly God. The Eucharistic species remind us that bread and wine are gifts of the Creator, given us anew by our Redeemer. "Blessed are you, Lord, God of all creation. Through your goodness we have this bread to offer . . . this wine to offer. . . . "

If we have a truly Eucharistic memory whereby we relive the Paschal Mystery, we have also a new, redeemed perception of bread and wine. They stand for all the gifts of creation, and we honor them as God's gifts, given for all. This way of looking at the Eucharistic sharing of God's gifts provides us with a new insight on the manner we earn our bread (income) in daily life.

"I shall be with you"

The Eucharist is the most remarkable manifestation of Jesus' *advent* and *presence* in our midst. It is therefore important that we understand the specific dimensions of this presence. It is absolutely real, even more real than our personal presence to each other here on earth.

On the cross, Jesus is signally present to his Father, entrusting himself to the Father, knowing that he is the acceptable offering. He is really present to his Mother, who stands beneath the cross. He reaches out to her with strong and tender love, addressing her, entrusting his beloved disciple and, indeed, all of us to her. He is present in an astonishing way to the criminal crucified with him, assuring him of everlasting presence in paradise. And he is present to those who, by their sins, have crucified him: "Father, forgive!" All this is proof of his compelling presence, empowered by the Holy Spirit, who enables and anoints him to be with us as total gift of himself.

Jesus' presence in the Eucharistic memorial matches perfectly his sacrificial presence on the cross. It vividly manifests his sacrificial presence in the Paschal Mystery. In a special way it is the presence of Jesus' sacrificial love for us. He stands before the Father as the acceptable sacrifice, interceding for us.

He is with us in his celestial fullness, in the final glory of his all-embracing, self-giving love, although in a sacramentally indicated and hidden form. Through this sacramental presence, Jesus affirms that he died for us, continues to live for us in the present, and will be with us forever. His presence as abiding gift is a great challenge for us to respond by giving ourselves to him as freely as he offered himself on the cross.

But his presence offers us infinitely more than a mere moral challenge. To those who believe in him he offers the power of the Holy Spirit who grants them the courage to give themselves as total gift to Jesus and, with him, to the Father. Thus they share actively in Jesus' and the Father's love for all their brothers and sisters. The Eucharist also offers a new range of vision for viewing our own human presence — our being with and for each other.

The real presence of the Eucharistic Lord is directly connected with his sacrifice. Jesus' presence is absolute and unconditional, but our response depends on the degree to which we are actually present to him and to each other in a sacrifical love, ready to renounce whatever hinders such a love.

The divine presence of Jesus is realized in the established realm of love to which only the loving belong. He is our ultimate destiny. By permitting the Holy Spirit to shape our memory into a truly grateful one in this memorial, we allow the Spirit to make us into an acceptable gift in return for Jesus' presence throughout our lives. His presence brings with it the life-giving Spirit. Those who refuse the gift and challenge of this life-giving Spirit cut themselves off from the saving presence of the Eucharistic Lord.

In the Eucharistic memorial, the Church, by the power of the Holy Spirit, places on the altar the sacramental signs of the sacrifice of Christ, knowing that the Father endorses Jesus' redemptive love. The real presence of Jesus in the Eucharist reminds us of what he did for us and what he is for us.

By positioning sacramentally on the altar the Lamb who died for us and who stands before the Father rendering thanks, praising, and interceding for us all, the Church, emphasizes the trinitarian reality of the Eucharistic presence. By the power of the Holy Spirit, and with Christ and the Father, she sends her love out into the world. She encourages people to open themselves to this vision and to do away with everything that stands in the way of this kind of being-present — all this in loving obedience to the Father, who wants all his children to be truly present to him in a mutual manifestation of Christlike love for each other.

The real presence of the risen Lord in the Eucharist is a mystery calling for reverence, awe, and adoration; it belies any kind of philosophical "explanation." Yet, for the believer, the vital dimensions of this privileged Eucharistic presence can be examined in view of challenge and response.

a) Real presence implies personal communication. Christ's presence in the Eucharist points to the most sublime communication and, above all, to *Communion*. It involves the Church and each believing participant in a loving communication with the Father. Through Communion we are ushered into the mutual love between the Father and the incarnate Son in the power of the Holy Spirit. The Spirit not only communicates to us the powerful message that Christ died for us, but also makes us sharers in his love so that, in Christ, we can love God with God's love and love each other with the Father's and Christ's love.

b) The glorified Christ is with the Father, *in his glory as God-Man*. He comes to us in the Eucharist and abides with us in order to lead us finally into the same presence *in the glory of the Father*. Jesus' presence is dynamic, powerfully shaping our final presence, our final home in God.

c) Christ has chosen bread and wine as sacramental signs for his nourishing presence, thereby implying to his Church and his disciples that he, himself, is the nourishing love and presence on our pilgrim way. He also empowers us to become effective signs of nourishing love for each other in human and spiritual needs.

God's real presence, meant to nourish a person's faith, hope, and love, calls for self-examination on the part of the recipient. It is a great challenge. Everyone "must test himself before eating his share of the bread and drinking from the cup'' (1 Corinthians 11:28). Whoever "eats this bread" while refusing true faith and love is desecrating the real presence of Jesus, and condemns himself to exile from him.

d) Christ is present on earth in this distinctive way by the *epiclesis,* the Church's calling on the power of the Holy Spirit before, during, and after the words by which Jesus instituted the Eucharistic memorial. The Spirit (through this liturgical invocation) descends upon the offering — the bread and wine — at the time of the consecration, to make them signs of Jesus' life-giving presence. The Church also calls the Holy Spirit to come upon the participants so that, in a spirit of generous response they may be in communion with the Lord and in communication with each other.

e) Christ is present to nourish his Church, to build up his mystical body in unity, love, and solidarity. We make a genuine response if we long to become constructive members of Christ's body, the Church.

"This is my body given for you, my blood shed for you"

The very words of the institution of the Eucharist turn our attention to the sacrifice wherein Christ, on the cross, offered himself for our salvation. The memorial, celebrated in the form of a meal, is a sharing in the death which Christ suffered for us and an entering into his sacrificing, reconciling love.

Authorized by Christ himself and in the power of the Holy Spirit, the Church proclaims the death and Resurrection of Christ. She is assured, and assures her believers, that Christ gives himself at Communion with the same love that he manifested by his death on the cross. We praise him for that abiding, life-giving love by being ready to put to death in ourselves whatever might be an obstacle to the same kind of love. It is inconceivable that we could participate in the sacrifice of praise without being ready to conquer in ourselves the poisoning powers of selfishness, violence, pride, and arrogance. With the whole Church we pray to God, in the Eucharistic memorial, to help us to appreciate ever more his work of redemption and to relive the Paschal Mystery of his cruel death and glorious Resurrection for the salvation of the world.

Eucharistic veneration, in all its dimensions and aspects, turns our grateful attention to the Cross to enable us, by faith in the Resurrection, to bear our burdens in the same spirit as Christ bore his cross for us. The sacrificial death — into which we enter by Communion — and the whole Eucharistic celebration involve no physical death; but it sets in motion the on-going process of putting to death any selfish and sensual tendencies. At the same time it also reminds us of the hour of our death and gives us the courage and strength to unite our dying with the redeeming death of Christ, and to rejoice in the hope of resurrection.

As fruit of the Eucharistic sacrifice and of Communion with the body of Christ scourged for us and the blood of Christ shed for us, we can say with Saint Paul: "It is now my happiness to suffer for you. This is my way of helping to complete, in my poor flesh, the full tale of Christ's afflictions still to be endured, for the sake of his body which is the church" (Colossians 1:24).

"Lamb of God, you take away the sins of the world"

A dimension of the Eucharist and of all forms of Eucharistic worship which deserves particular attention is indicated by the prayer, "Lamb of God, you take away the sins of the world: have mercy on us . . . grant us peace."

This prayer reminds us not so much of the Paschal lamb of the Exodus, when the Passover was instituted (Exodus 12), as of the songs of the Servant and his peace mission:

"On himself he bore our sufferings,
    our torments he endured,
while we counted him smitten by God,
    struck down by disease and misery;
but he was pierced for our transgressions,
    tortured for our iniquities;
the chastisement he bore is health for us
    and by his scourging we are healed.
We had all strayed like sheep,
each of us had gone his own way;
but the LORD laid upon him
    the guilt of us all.
He was afflicted, he submitted to be struck down
    and did not open his mouth;
he was led like a sheep to the slaughter,
like a ewe that is dumb before the shearers. . . .
He had done no violence
    and spoken no word of treachery.
Yet the LORD took thought for his tortured servant
    and healed him who had made himself a sacrifice for
        sin . . . .
He bore the sin of many
    and interceded for their transgressions"
(Isaiah 53:4-7,9-10,12).

The New Testament leaves no doubt that Jesus was and understood himself explicitly to be that Servant of whom the four songs speak: the Servant who suffers like a lamb and by his gentleness breaks the deadly circle of violence. He bears the horrifying burden of the world's transgressions, and opens the way for a saving solidarity and *peace*. At the baptism of Jesus in the Jordan, "a voice from heaven was heard saying, 'This is my Son, my Beloved, on whom my favour rests' " (Matthew 3:17). These words clearly point to the first verse of the first song of the Servant (Isaiah 42:1). And it is John the Baptizer who points to Jesus, saying: "There is the Lamb of God; it is he who takes away the sin of the world" (John 1:29).

The whole Eucharistic memorial exhorts us to "behold the Lamb of God!" It urges us to learn from him who is meek, nonviolent, humble, and thus points out the way of peace. The Lamb "with the marks of slaughter upon him" (Revelation 5:6) is "worthy to take the scroll and to break its seals" (Revelation 5:9) to reveal the deepest meaning of the history of salvation. The Eucharist brings the pilgrim Church into the heavenly liturgy: "Victory to our God who sits on the throne, and to the Lamb" (Revelation 7:10). The Lamb of God turns our eyes and hearts to his ways of loving forgiveness. He rescues even his enemies, the sinners, by his life and death; he shows us the healing power of nonviolence as the expression of redeeming love for those who oppose him and his disciples.

The deepest meaning of Christ's sin-offering, which we celebrate in the Eucharist, is not the payment of a debt imposed by vindictive justice but, rather, the bearing of the burden of all sinners; it is thus a call to total conversion. He alone, in whom there is no violence and no treachery, can deliver us from the solidarity of sin and lead us into the solidarity of salvation.

Devotion to the Eucharist should open our eyes to the Redeemer's nonviolence, and particularly to nonviolence as the healing response to humanity's present madness, which claims that the mutual threat of total annihilation is the way to peace. The Eucharist does not present ready solutions to the terrible problems caused by the arms race of the superpowers and their satellites. But we can learn much about peace by listening with our hearts to the Lamb of God whose final victory we celebrate in the Eucharist. By his body given for us and his blood shed for us, we develop an effective love for all our neighbors and especially for those who are enemies of patient nonviolence and absolute truthfulness.

"This is the cup of my blood, the blood of the new and everlasting covenant"

By shedding his own blood, not that of others or of scapegoats (as in Old Testament sacrifices), Jesus seals the new and everlasting covenant of a saving solidarity. Sharing in Christ's body given for us and his blood shed for us, we enter into this covenant expressed by a love that will never become disordered.

Saint Augustine, time and again, wrote of his tremendous vision: to receive the body of Christ and become the body of Christ — a fitting member, a supportive member, ready to make all the sacrifices needed for keeping and fostering the bonds of unity and peace! When we share faithfully in the cup of the new covenant, we endorse the "law of Christ" written in our hearts: "Help one another to carry these heavy loads, and in this way you will fulfil the law of Christ" (Galatians 6:2).

Eucharistic worship is authentic if all our thinking and all our human relationships confirm our membership in this community of salvation. It is unthinkable to live covenant solidarity only on the level of devotion. We, who receive in the Eucharist the Word of God and the body and blood of Christ as signs of redemption, must show a redeemed attitude in dealing with earthly goods. Christians of wealthy industrial nations will prove that they have benefited from Eucharistic worship when they begin to recognize that unfair monopolies are often the cause of many national and international socio-economic problems.

Sharing on all levels is, in a certain sense, "natural" for Christians who know what they receive and what they celebrate in the Eucharist.

"So that sins may be forgiven"

There are many avenues of divine forgiveness, liturgical and extra-liturgical. In the first place there is Baptism. " 'Repent,' said Peter, 'repent and be baptized, every one of you, in the name of Jesus the Messiah for the forgivenesss of your sins' " (Acts 2:38). There is also a dimension of forgiveness of sins in the sacrament of Anointment of the Sick. "Is anyone among you in trouble? . . . He should send for the elders of the congregation to pray over him and anoint him with oil in the name of the Lord. The prayer offered in faith will save the sick man, the Lord will raise him from his bed, and any sins he may have committed will be forgiven. Therefore confess your sins to one another, and pray for one another, and then you will be healed. A good man's prayer is powerful and effective" (James 5:13-16). James' text on the Anointment of the Sick is also preceded by a strong warning: "Do not blame your troubles on one another, or you will fall under judgment" (James 5:9).

All sacramental and nonsacramental ways of obtaining forgiveness of sins from God imply the condition expressed in the Lord's prayer: "Forgive us our trespasses as we forgive those who trespass against us." The forgiveness and reconciliation offered graciously by God call for total reconciliation: peace with God, with individuals, and among nations.

Forgiveness finds its center in the Paschal Mystery of Christ's death and Resurrection, which we celebrate in the Eucharistic memorial; it is this celebration which introduces us ever more completely to God's love. We listen to Jesus' prayer on the cross, offered for all of us: "Father, forgive!" From these words the healing power of the gospel of peace and reconciliation emanate. And from them we learn the gentle "law of grace," whereby we meet each other in healing, forgiving love — especially those who, by their enmity and violence, are in special need of such love and reconciliation.

Our access to the saving and healing dimension of the Eucharist reminds us how much we need healing, forgiving grace. "If we claim to be sinless, we are self-deceived and strangers to the truth. If we confess our sins, he is just, and may be trusted to forgive our sins and cleanse us from every kind of wrong; but if we say we have committed no sin, we make him out to be a liar, and then his word has no place in us" (1 John 1:8-10).

The entire Eucharistic liturgy reminds us of our need to be forgiven and the importance of starting life anew. Right at the beginning we confess our sins as a group. Then the proclamation of the Word of God and the priest's homily serve to make us more aware of our need to be more open to God's healing forgiveness.

During the early centuries, in many areas of the Church, the first part of Mass provided a time for general confession of sins and general absolution. But those who had committed gravely scandalous sins were not allowed to receive Communion without previous reconciliation through the sacrament of Penance. The Communion rite has no less than three prayers that focus on forgiveness: the "Our Father," the "Deliver us, Lord, from every evil" (marking sin as the greatest evil), and "Lamb of God, you take away the sins of the world: have mercy on us." Then, before receiving Communion we humbly acknowledge once more our need of healing forgiveness: "Lord, I am not worthy. . . . "

All these prayers seeking forgiveness together with our readiness to forgive one another as the Lord God forgives us are brought into the realm of the Eucharist: to praise and thank God for his healing action in Christ, our Redeemer, and to thank Jesus who gave himself up for us "so that sins may be forgiven."

Thus the Eucharist enkindles in us that love of God and neighbor that banishes fear and erases sin.

"Mystery of Faith"

The Eucharist is the summit of our religious existence. The whole life of the Church derives from it and leads to it. Above all, it is the supreme expression and celebration of the Church's faith, the precious "sacrament of faith," through which the faith of the community nourishes and strengthens the faith of each participant. It is and should be an ever more joyous, grateful celebration of faith, filled with hope which in turn bears fruit in love for the life of the world.

In the Eucharist the Lord feeds us with his Word, meditated on and celebrated by the faith-community, in preparation for nourishment with his body and blood. Both his Word and his Body are the bread from heaven which can bring us to the fullness of faith and a life worthy of the children of God. This point has great ecumenical relevance.

The Second Vatican Council's liturgical renewal — especially the use of the vernacular for the proclamation of the Word of God — has torn down many barriers between Catholics and people of other faiths who desire to understand our faith in the Eucharist in its various dimensions.

The evident vitality exhibited by a Christian community celebrating "the mystery of faith" is definite proof of the excellence of the Eucharist. This has been proven time and again. Some years ago I conducted some sociological pastoral researches on this point. In scattered areas of various dioceses I sought information about differences in the manner of celebrating the Eucharist, taking into consideration the sociological composition of the congregations. I studied parishes which followed the strict Latin rite with no active participation by the faithful in contrast to parishes where active participation by the faithful was encouraged by proper instruction.

The contrast was enormous. Where only the strict Latin liturgy obtained, attendance showed a shocking absence of young adults and males of almost all age groups. Blue-collar workers also stayed away in droves; and the rate of divorce was high in conjunction with the low number of children per family. In the same area, with almost the same sociological conditions, a lively celebration of the liturgy in the vernacular, coupled with more openness between the priest and the laity, attracted up to three times more men, more young adults. It also seemed to have an evident impact on the thinking of the parishioners: their attitudes about the number of children per family, about abortion, and about divorce were much more Christ-like.

Other studies have shown that, in parishes where the proclamation of the Word of God and a joyous celebration of faith were not overshadowed by a disturbing emphasis on money-raising, people usually showed much more generosity for the needs of the Church and the poor.

The various forms of sound Eucharistic devotions other than the Mass itself are highly relevant for deepening and strengthening faith. The Eucharistic celebration itself becomes, then, the summit and fruitful source of a life of faith active in love.

"Every time you eat this bread and drink this cup, you proclaim the death of the Lord, until he comes"

Christ can be present in all the Masses celebrated throughout the world because he is in the glory of the Father. He has attained his final purpose and destiny. The Lamb, slaughtered as sin-offering for our sins, fulfills the saving plan to reconcile the universe through his death and reigns forever over heaven and earth. In him, all of redeemed humanity and, indeed, the whole cosmos have their center. He is the One who came, who continues to come, and will never cease coming. The One who is present in the Eucharist is specifically the One in whom the final fulfillment is already fully anticipated.

Among many other consequences of this, two are outstanding. We proclaim his death in the light of resurrection and final glory; therefore, we can face our mortality with conviction and the hour of our death with calmness. Living on the level of the Eucharist, we will never repress the thought of our mortality; the prospect of our death does not torment us. And the other consequence is that we cannot proclaim his death and think about the death of his disciples without seeing and facing death in the light of ultimate fulfillment, in the light of that mysterious reality which we witness in the Eucharist. There can be no gap between *Anamnesis* and *prolepsis,* between remembrance of the saving deed of the past and anticipation-expectation of the final coming of Christ, of the new heaven and the new earth.

Clearly, the Eucharistic celebration and the life of Christians marked by veneration of the Eucharist allow us to pray with great confidence, yearning, and joy: "Come, Lord Jesus!" (Revelation 22:20)

In the Eucharist we celebrate past and future in the heart of *presence:* Jesus' presence and his way of making present his and our future. The Father sends the Son who fulfills his mission of glory. Facing the horrifying moment when he, the Lamb of God, will have to make himself a sin-offering by his nonviolent, liberating response to human violence, Jesus prays: "Now my soul is in turmoil, and what am I to say?" Shall I say, " 'Father, save me from this hour? No, it was for this that I came to this hour. Father, glorify thy name.' A voice sounded from heaven: 'I have glorified it, and I will glorify it again' " (John 12:27-28).

And for him the very glorification of the Lamb enthroned in heaven is his Eucharistic mission, signifying his desire for us through and in the proclamation of his death, Resurrection, and Ascension into heaven. As in the heavenly liturgy of the Lamb, so in the Eucharist, the celebration of the Paschal Mystery reminds us of the final coming of the Lord and the final fulfillment of redemption and glorification.

For Jesus, death and resurrection are the final homecoming to the Father. The Eucharist is a sacramental assurance for Christ's disciples that he has prepared for them their eternal home in the glory of the Father. This vision in no way compromises our earthly mission. Rather, it provides us with a powerful dynamic for our mission — so that we can "use the present opportunity to the full" (Ephesians 5:15).

The author of the Letter to the Hebrews points all this out in a powerful way. "It is by the will of God that we have been consecrated, through the offering of the body of Jesus Christ once and for all. . . . Christ offered for all time one sacrifice for sins, and took his seat at the right hand of God. . . . For by one offering he has perfected for all time those who are thus consecrated. . . . So now, my friends, the blood of Jesus makes us free to enter boldly into the sanctuary by the new, living way which he has opened for us through the curtain, the way of his flesh. . . . Let us make our approach in sincerity of heart and full of assurance of faith" (Hebrews 10:10-22). "Let us therefore boldly approach the throne of our gracious God, where we may receive mercy and in his grace find timely help" (Hebrews 4:16).

"Adorers in spirit and in truth"

One of the awe-inspiring facts in Jesus' life was that he chose to disclose to a Samaritan woman — a person despised on several grounds — a major dimension of his mission. "The time approaches, indeed it is already here, when those who are real worshippers will worship the Father in spirit and in truth. Such are the worshippers whom the Father wants. God is spirit, and those who worship him must worship in spirit and in truth" (John 4:23-24).

In Jesus, the Father's design is fulfilled. He stands forever before the throne of the Father in his Paschal reality, offering himself in his saving, self-giving love. Forever he is the acceptable sacrifice. Through him, in the name of all humanity and of all creation, the Father receives adoration "in spirit and in truth."

It is Jesus' Eucharistic mission — his whole mission — to bring the redeemed into the realm of adoration in spirit and truth. His mission is completed in his Paschal Mystery and in his everlasting presence before the throne of our gracious God. Through our adoration in spirit and truth he makes us partners in his saving love and his work of redemption. In the Eucharist he urges us from within (living in us and with us) to unite ourselves with him, in adoration — the same kind of adoration which the Father is offered eternally by the Lamb standing before his throne.

When we celebrate the Eucharist devoutly, we let the Holy Spirit consecrate us to the loving will of God. And on our part, we dedicate ourselves — our memory, heart, mind, intelligence, and will — to him, who so graciously gives his body and blood, his whole self as gift to us.

This is the spirit of adoration that marks Eucharistic worship.

III

Fostering Eucharistic Devotions

We preserve the soundness of our faith by making careful distinctions between the abiding truth of revelation and the time-honored expression of that truth. And we do this in the faith community under the guidance of the teaching authority of the Church.

It is impossible always and everywhere to preserve the customs and traditions of our faith without some kind of adaptation. We have to live our traditional faith in the present moment of history, and try our best to transmit it to our contemporaries in vigorous and assertive terms.

Cultures, societies, communities, economies, and politics change in accord with people's way of thinking and acting. And, as members of today's Church, we share the gifts of the Father, Son, and Holy Spirit with the same faithful commitment as our ancestors did, although in slightly different forms which are necessitated by new conditions.

Having reviewed the history of Eucharistic devotion and the main dimensions of the Eucharistic memorial, we now turn to the ways in which we can foster Eucharistic devotion in our present day. Our purpose is to reawaken true Eucharistic piety in today's world.

All the sacraments of the New Covenant open up new horizons of grace, each one demanding proper preparation and reflective acceptance of its specific grace and direction. But there is a need to cultivate a specific spirituality relating to our Lord's permanent presence in the Eucharist. It is impossible to ignore his gracious call to "be what you see and receive what you are called for! Let Christ live in your heart, mind, will, and life!"

The core of Eucharistic piety is frequent remembrance of past, present, and future celebrations of the Mass: its meaning for our lives, for our concerns, endeavors, and relationships. We express this devotion in an ideal way when — before Mass — we prepare our minds and hearts for the event and — after Mass — we reflect on how, during the day or week, we can express and foster the abiding gratitude which this Eucharistic memorial evokes.

Those who attend Sunday Mass and then during the ensuing week forget what they have celebrated and received are acting irrationally. The main purpose of our Eucharistic worship is to establish an ever better alliance between receiving and giving, contemplation and action, divine rites and human rights, reverence for the mystery of holiness and familiarity with Jesus, the God-Man. Only in this way will we overcome the gap between religion and daily life.

Sound Eucharistic piety and sound Eucharistic devotions should also help us eliminate present dangerous polarizations in the Church, particularly those surrounding Eucharistic spirituality and liturgical forms. This is one of the main concerns of this booklet.

The Instruction on the Eucharistic Mystery (issued by the Holy See in 1967) and the apostolic letter of John Paul II (issued in 1980) ''On the Mystery and the Worship of the Eucharist'' encourage the following forms of Eucharistic piety: celebration of the feast of Corpus Christi and its solemn procession, Eucharistic congresses, shorter or longer periods of exposition of the Blessed Sacrament with solemn Benediction, annual celebration of forty hours of adoration, other hours of adoration, perpetual adoration in dioceses, and, last but not least, silent prayer before the tabernacle.

In all these devotional ways of fostering a Eucharistic spirituality, we never lose sight of the center and summit of Christian life: the celebration of the Eucharistic memorial (the Mass) with the reception of Holy Communion.

Corpus Christi

Around the year 1209, a group of holy women in Liège, Belgium, established a center dedicated to Eucharistic piety. These women were convinced that the Lord desired a new feast — that of Corpus Christi — dedicated to the reserved Sacrament of the Altar. For this feast, Thomas Aquinas, one of the greatest theologians of all ages, composed beautiful hymns that expertly combined dogma with devotion.

With its rich Eucharistic liturgy and procession, the feast of Corpus Christi is an occasion of special praise and thanksgiving offered to the Father in the name of all creation, and of special thanksgiving for the institution of the Eucharist in which Christ's body is the bread of life. It is an extension of the praise expressed in its very institution: "On the night he was betrayed, he took bread and gave you thanks and praise. . . . When supper was ended, he took the cup. Again he gave you thanks and praise."

Saint Augustine taught that eternal life is essentially praise and thanksgiving and that, therefore, a life lived in grateful praise is really the road to final fulfillment. The feast of Corpus Christi was and is, in many parts of the Catholic Church, a unique occasion for creative forms of praise and thanksgiving.

The Corpus Christi procession is a solemn act of public adoration and praise; it is in perfect harmony with the Eucharistic memorial. In Catholic towns all the houses are decorated for this procession. There is an abundance of flowers everywhere, especially before the four altars where the Gospels are sung and solemn Benediction is given. And amidst these beautiful artistic arrangements of flowers, church choirs and music makers of all kinds perform at their best. Members of various associations, wearing their distinctive garb, add vivid color to the occasion. All this activity points to praise of the Creator. And it is all done freely and generously. The Corpus Christi procession is a kind of cosmic liturgy. Symbolically it invites all creatures to join in the Church's joy, gratitude, and praise. Thus, festivity and solemnity combine to mark this Eucharistic celebration and procession.

Solemn Benediction is also a feature of the procession. At each altar, after the singing of the Gospel and special prayers calling for the Lord's blessing on the four corners of the earth, there is a solemn blessing with the Blessed Sacrament in the monstrance. The prayer of praise and thanksgiving is, itself, a blessing coming from God, opening our hearts for renewed graces. Ordinarily, when we bless others on various occasions, we invoke Almighty God. At the solemn Eucharistic Benediction, it is more evident that Christ himself blesses us and intends to make all of us a blessing for each other. And this we are, if all our life is marked by a spirit of joyous faith and praise.

Church processions, but particularly the Corpus Christi procession, symbolize among other things our pilgrimage on the road to our final destination with Christ accompanying us; for he is the Way and at the same time our final Home.

The feast of Corpus Christi, with its solemn procession, was most popular in times and areas where all were Catholics, grateful for the gift of faith and particularly for their faith in the Eucharist. Thanks be to God, there are still places where this is the case even today.

I vividly remember how we celebrated the feast of Corpus Christi in Poland back in 1945. After years of repression, the people were once again allowed their beloved Eucharistic procession. Not only did they celebrate the feast with joyful song, but during the procession they wept for joy. They wanted everyone to know how happy they were to once again be able to publicly profess their faith.

Eucharistic congresses on the national and international levels may be compared to feasts of Corpus Christi on an enlarged scale. Drawing vast crowds, they serve as powerful inspiration for the restoration of Eucharistic veneration and — especially during the last decades — for liturgical renewal. The latest national and international congresses have exemplified how traditional forms of Eucharistic devotion can be easily adapted to the liturgical renewal demanded by the Second Vatican Council — and this without any detriment to its former popular appeal. And, although the first Eucharistic congresses met vehement opposition from Protestant churches, the more recent congresses are not without a certain ecumenical attraction. This is due not only to the Catholic liturgical renewal but also to a new openness in other areas of Christianity.

Solemn Exposition
of the Blessed Sacrament

The rubric of elevating the Host after consecration and the custom of Eucharistic processions arose because of the people's desire to see the consecrated Host. They were inspired with awe at the self-effacing humility of the Lord of glory, and they were filled with joy at the sight of this sacramental sign of his abiding presence. Thus began a rich development of various forms of public adoration.

In the fourteenth century, the exposition of the Blessed Sacrament in the monstrance was a popular evening devotion. Then came what is called the Forty Hours Devotion, in which our Lord's presence in the Eucharist is honored, sermons on the Blessed Sacrament are preached, and solemn sacramental Benediction is given. In Germany during this period, the devotion was so popular that the exposition of the Blessed Sacrament was held during the whole year, either in specific churches or chapels or so scheduled that there was always this special service, this uninterrupted "great prayer," in one of the churches of a diocese. Papal delegates repeatedly imposed restrictions, but the movement was very persistent. It came from the hearts of the people and was implemented by zealous priests. After the Council of Trent, the solemn exposition in the monstrance, which had previously been restricted in most countries to the feast of Corpus Christi, was promoted everywhere.

"Forty hours of prayer" was an ancient tradition in the whole Church, in remembrance of Jesus' forty days in the desert. And from the sixteenth century on, the forty hours of prayer before the Blessed Sacrament exposed in the monstrance became even more popular. In 1539, Paul III favored the practice by granting a special indulgence. Saint Charles Borromeo confirmed the practice for Milan in the Synod of 1565 and extended it to the whole province of Milan in 1575. Urban VIII then extended this solemn adoration to the whole Western Church. It surely served as inspiration for many Christians and Christian communities.

As a young priest, I witnessed in several parishes a kind of Eucharistic fervor in the people at the time of Forty Hours Devotion. The church was crowded for all the Masses and almost all the parishioners received the sacraments of Penance and Holy Communion. It was an annual renewal of the community. It would be a pity to let it die out.

These forms of Eucharistic devotion not only affirm our faith in the real presence of Christ in the Blessed Sacrament; they educate us in the practice of adoration, praise, and thanksgiving.

Adoration of our Lord's humble presence is an antidote to atheism and secularism, and a civilization with an unbalanced emphasis on human achievement. While it has the power to heal the withdrawal of those lost in the "lonely crowd," it does not divert us from our responsibilities in and for the world. If, in adoration we learn to let God be God in all our concerns, we shall also be able to let the world be world without allowing it to corrupt us in any way.

Reverence for the Viaticum

Through the centuries, the main reason for reservation of the Blessed Sacrament has been care for the Viaticum. In the beginning, the Blessed Sacrament was brought to the sick and the dying by the priest immediately after the Eucharistic celebration. This was done to preserve the connection between the Mass and our Lord's Divine Presence which is a direct result of the Eucharistic celebration. But this method changed through the years. At one period, the Blessed Sacrament was brought either by members of the sick person's family or by a deacon. Also, there were times when family members were allowed to care for its preservation so that the sick person could receive Communion explicitly as Viaticum as soon as he or she felt death approaching. It has always been a matter of great concern to the Church that the sick have access to the Viaticum and to frequent Communion during long-lasting illness.

As early as the thirteenth century, the faithful, carrying candles in their hands, were invited to accompany the Blessed Sacrament from the church to the house of the sick person, in a kind of Eucharistic procession. In those days, people were always happy to do this. In rural Catholic communities where more leisure time was available for devotional practices, this custom caused no problems. The faithful would appear at least at the doorways of their houses to receive the sacramental blessing.

However times may change, the wonderful fact that Jesus remains in the Blessed Sacrament, ever ready to console the sick, should enkindle special devotion, gratitude, and adoration. It also should be and, indeed, is for many believers a strong motive to share in Jesus' love for the sick and dying.

If possible, the whole family should gather and welcome the Lord when the Blessed Sacrament is brought to the sick in the home. Great care should be taken that sick persons are given the opportunity to receive Holy Communion frequently, and especially that those in danger of death receive the Viaticum while still fully conscious.

In view of the shortage of priests and deacons, qualified people — often senior citizens — can render valuable services in caring for the lonely and sick by loving care and prayerful assistance. In many Catholic parishes these good people are entrusted with this special ministry: They bring the Blessed Sacrament to the sick for whom they also care in other ways. And, at the proper time, they inform the pastor when those under their care should receive the Anointment of the Sick. At that time they not only prepare the room with table, cross, and candles, but they also patiently pray with words of faith and comfort for fruitful reception of the sacraments. It would be good for us to practice some of these old traditions.

Private Visits
to the Blessed Sacrament

Time spent reflecting in the presence of Jesus Christ is time gratefully accepted from the Lord of history, who graces us here on earth with his loving presence. It is time that merits for us eternal life.

People who think they are too busy should listen to the call, "Awake, sleeper, rise from the dead, and Christ will shine upon you" (Ephesians 5:14). If we become thankfully aware of Christ's presence, he — the one who is light of the world and wants to make us, in him and with him, light for the world — alerts our senses to a fuller life, to the true light. From this short exposure to Christ in our visits to the Blessed Sacrament, there arises also a sharper awareness of the preciousness of time: "Use the present opportunity to the full" (Ephesians 5:16).

A priest in Zaire asked a young man, whom he saw spending hours before the tabernacle: "What do you do all this time?" The response was simple: "I let my soul enjoy the sunshine!"

To better utilize this time in God's presence it might be well to pursue the following objectives.

Adore God

The burning lamp near the tabernacle says to us: Remember the gracious nearness of Jesus who came like a candle to bring warmth, peace, and light into the world, and spent himself finally on the cross to enter into the fullness of the Father's glory.

Before the tabernacle we adore the eternal Word who took flesh, became one of us to enlighten everyone. In adoration of the mystery of God's condescendence, our faith in the Paschal Mystery lifts our hearts, and we meditate on the word of the Seer of Patmos: "I was caught up by the Spirit. There in heaven stood a throne, and on the throne sat one whose appearance was like a gleam of jasper and cornelian;

and round the throne was a rainbow, bright as an emerald.
. . . Then I saw standing in the very middle of the throne,
inside the circle of living creatures and the circle of elders, a
Lamb with the marks of slaughter upon him'' (Revelation
4:2; 5:6). Turning our eyes and hearts to these marks, we say
with Thomas: ''My Lord and my God!''

The Lamb standing before the Father's throne is the eternal
intercessor. The Father remembers forever that his Son-
made-Man bears these marks for us, thus ''calling to mind
his solemn covenant'' (Luke 1:72).

Silent adoration before the tabernacle is a wholesome
remembrance, a kind of training for a healthy, grateful
memory that brings us closer to the Faithful One who
remembers us by his gracious presence in our midst.

To make more fruitful our time of remembrance before the
tabernacle or monstrance, here are two suggestions. One is to
meditate from time to time on the official Eucharistic prayers
of the Mass, word by word. Letting the words enter deeply
into our hearts, we will experience the depth and wealth of
these texts with greater joy during our next participation in
the Mass.

The other suggestion is that, in the presence of Jesus who
stands before the Father as the Lamb marked by the signs of
slaughter, we meditate on all the great mysteries of creation:
the Incarnation of the Word of God, the Passion, death,
Resurrection, and Ascension into heaven of Jesus, and the
descent of the Holy Spirit on his Church. Then, thus re-
minded, we examine our own life history and lead it, point by
point, into thanksgiving for the countless blessings we have
received. We don't leave out our disappointments, our sufferings or daily crosses; we try to fit them into the whole picture
as they blend with the Lamb marked by the signs of slaughter.
We then praise the Lord who, through his death, his Resur-

rection, and his Eucharistic union with us, has given our wounds a new meaning for ourselves and for others.

As we sit or kneel before the tabernacle, we should be ever thankful that so many happenings, which for unbelievers prove to be sheer frustration, make sense for believers who begin to share in the history of salvation because they are living in profound union with the Holy Redeemer.

Whisper: "Lord, here I am!"

Before the self-giving presence of Jesus in the Blessed Sacrament we remember the many times when he nourished our faith, hope, and love with his body and his blood. By giving himself to us, he encourages us to give ourselves to him. Our reflective adoration before the Sacrament of Abiding Presence becomes a prayer of readiness *now:* "Lord, here I am! Accept me! Transform me! Send me!" And we begin to examine the critical areas of our daily life: our relationships with our neighbors, with those who misunderstand us, with those who oppose us, with those who need greater love and affirmation from us, and with those who need our healing and reconciling love.

In his letter "On the Mystery and Worship of the Eucharist," John Paul II writes: "This veneration arises from love and fosters the love to which we are called." Let us, then, constantly pray to "the Lamb marked with the signs of slaughter" for the same kind of love that he has shown us. He died for us sinners, offered himself up for us who, by our sins, have rebelled against him. On the cross he cried out to the Father for us, "Father, forgive! They do not realize what they are doing."

By creating a new life within us at Holy Communion, he calls us to imitate his kind of love. In this light, we take a new look at our relationships with those who have hurt us or those whom we have hurt. We pray to Jesus to conform our hearts to his, to strengthen us with a healing, reconciling love. We celebrate the Eucharist for the forgiveness of sins. Should we not also pray frequently before the tabernacle: "Lord, heal us, for we have sinned against you," and thus open ourselves to the charism of healing love that will wipe out all hatred?

And as we bring our personal experiences, our individual needs, and all our hurts to Jesus in the Blessed Sacrament, we cannot forget that the object of our adoration is "the Lamb of God who takes upon himself the burden of the sin of the world," the Peacemaker who prevails over violence. In his presence, our prayer, "Lord, here I am!" becomes mission and readiness to make our best contribution for a peaceful world, a system of nonviolence everywhere and on all levels.

Try to understand God's will for you

We spend our time well before the tabernacle in silent prayer, meditation, and thanksgiving when, under the eyes of Jesus, the Lamb marked with the signs of slaughter, we try to discern what the will of God is for us. We know that we can do nothing for salvation by ourselves. Therefore, we should listen to the exhortation of the Apostle: "Let the Holy Spirit fill you" (Ephesians 5:18).

When we gratefully allow Jesus to "shine upon us" and illumine us by the mysteries which we meditate and glorify in this sacrament, we can be assured that the Holy Spirit will permeate us, guide us, and strengthen us. Our willing attitude puts us on the same wavelength with the Holy Spirit, who will help us to examine our desires, refine our plans, and analyze our capabilities so that we can sincerely offer them to Jesus as signs of our ardent gratitude. It is then that we begin to see clearly what we have to renounce and what we have to cultivate in ourselves and in our surroundings and lifestyles.

Pray to him:
"Come, Lord Jesus!"

We have seen that the sacramental presence of Jesus in the Eucharist is the Paschal Mystery reaching out to us. It is the Paschal Mystery made present by the coming of Jesus, who is the glory of the Father. Our Eucharistic veneration would be neither sound nor healing if we were to neglect this dimension. We look forward to the final coming of the Lord. '' 'Come!' say the Spirit and the Bride. 'Come!' let each hearer reply. Come forward, you who are thirsty; accept the water of life, a free gift to all who desire it'' (Revelation 22:17).

A genuine Eucharistic devotion causes us to long for the final coming of the Lord, to long for our homecoming and for the homing of all creation into the ultimate freedom of the children of our Father. God is infinitely generous and rich in his gifts. But the gift of freedom will be given only to those who desire it. Eucharistic worship helps us to free ourselves from useless desires and cares, and opens us to the living water that wells up for eternal life.

Our willingness to pray, "Lord, here I am!" and our effort to discern, in the presence of the Lord, what the will of God is, prepare us for our mission, our responsibility in the world. The more we listen to him who promises, "Yes, I am coming soon!" the more our manner of life responds: "Amen, come, Lord Jesus!" (Revelation 22:20)

Submit to him with the words: "Your kingdom come!"

Although we emphasize the importance of Eucharistic devotion here, we do so with no intention of "privatizing" religion. When we say with the Spirit, "Come!" we also pray with all our heart, "Your kingdom come!" Through Eucharistic veneration we enter more deeply into the dimensions of the kingdom of God, a kingdom of love, peace, and justice.

In silent contemplation and adoration before the Blessed Sacrament, before "the Lamb marked with slaughter upon him," we open ourselves to his liberating love, his saving justice, his forgiving mission. We speak to our Lord, "Here I am, send me!" And with a heart earnestly craving that the kingdom of God may reach all people, we pray that God's will be done. Letting our devotion shine before the world, we can hope that our actions will turn people's attention to the Lord when they see the good we do (see Matthew 5:16).

Conclusion

Almighty God, we thank you for giving us your beloved Son, our Redeemer. We can never praise you and your Son enough for the gift of the Eucharist.

We thank you for providing your Church in this century with a tremendous liturgical, Eucharistic renewal. Through Saint Pius X you have made it easier for all believers, including children, to receive Communion. Through Pius XII you have given us new access to the wealth and beauty of the celebration of Holy Week. Through the Second Vatican Council you have invited all the faithful to active participation in the Eucharistic celebration, and have impressed upon us the intimate unity of the liturgy of the Word and the liturgy of the Eucharist.

Throughout the whole Christian world you have sharpened our vision of the Eucharist as a great sacrament of unity, and have enkindled a strong desire to reach that level of unity in faith, hope, and love that would make it possible for all Christians to partake together of the Eucharistic banquet. In many areas of Christianity you have inspired a spirit of sacrifice and generosity that hopes to remove all the obstacles to a common celebration of the memorial of Christ's inimitable sacrifice.

Most believers today rejoice over the renewed Eucharistic liturgy. But there are many Catholics who, in spite of their appreciation, are unwilling to admit that regular participation in the Eucharist is a sign of grateful faith as well as necessary nourishment for blessed unity. There are others who are unwilling to open themselves to new horizons and to greater fidelity to the traditions of the Church. At the same time, there are many others who accept the renewal and gladly participate in the renewed Eucharistic celebration but are grieved because beloved Eucharistic devotions, once so fruitful for their lives of faith, have vanished in their area.

Lord, send forth your Spirit so that we may be not only more faithful to the liturgical heritage of the first Christian centuries but also may appreciate and cultivate the authentic and fruitful developments of the present and future Church.

Lord, grant us the spirit of discernment! Lord, make us faithful and grateful!

VISITS TO THE MOST BLESSED SACRAMENT AND THE BLESSED VIRGIN MARY

Prayers and meditations composed by Saint Alphonsus Liguori. $1.50

HEART OF JESUS: SYMBOL OF REDEEMING LOVE
by Bernard Häring, C.SS.R.

Thirty inspiring meditations on the Sacred Heart plus a short history that clearly shows how this devotion is based on the Bible and tradition. $4.95

MARY AND YOUR EVERYDAY LIFE
by Bernard Häring, C.SS.R.

Thirty-one simple meditations to help bring Mary and her Son into your daily life. $4.95

PRAYING TO GOD AS A FRIEND
*edited by the Immaculate Heart of Mary Sisters and
The Redemptorists*

This recent adaptation of Saint Alphonsus' classic "How to Converse Continually and Familiarly With God" contains brief prayers and reflections that are as valid today as when they were first written. $1.50

Order from your local bookstore or write to:
Liguori Publications
Box 060, Liguori, Missouri 63057-9999
*(Please add $1.00 for postage and handling for
orders under $5.00; $1.50 for orders over $5.00.)*